CAREER SUCCESS

Proven Strategies To Achieve Success In Your Career Fast

Introduction

I want to thank you and congratulate you for downloading this book.

The contents of this book has actionable information on how to attain career and life success by modifying your behavior to prime yourself for greatness in every area of your life.

Success is the dream of every living man and woman. Unfortunately, only a few actually achieve what they associate success with. Well, the truth is that the definition of success differs from person to person. For some, it's earning more money while others see it as spending more time with their family and for others, it is climbing to the top of the corporate ladder.

Regardless of your definition of success, you might wonder why you don't achieve it. You are not alone to think that. It's a question that more than 90% of the population ask from themselves but don't get the answer. A few years ago, I was also asking the same question from myself. But when I finally got the answer, I thought to write a book about it to help others who are stuck as I was to rocket fuel their success.

This book is about success, regardless of your definition of success. By reading this book, you will discover key behaviors that keep you from getting successful along with actionable information on how to adopt the right behaviors to put you back on the path to massive success in any area you wish to succeed. Let's begin.

Thanks again for downloading this book. I hope you enjoy it!

© Copyright 2018 - All rights reserved.

This document is geared towards providing exact and reliable information in regards to the topic and issue covered. The publication is sold with the idea that the publisher is not required to render accounting, officially permitted, or otherwise, qualified services. If advice is necessary, legal or professional, a practiced individual in the profession should be ordered.

- From a Declaration of Principles which was accepted and approved equally by a Committee of the American Bar Association and a Committee of Publishers and Associations.

In no way is it legal to reproduce, duplicate, or transmit any part of this document in either electronic means or in printed format. Recording of this publication is strictly prohibited and any storage of this document is not allowed unless with written permission from the publisher. All rights reserved.

The information provided herein is stated to be truthful and consistent, in that any liability, in terms of inattention or otherwise, by any usage or abuse of any policies, processes, or directions contained within is the solitary and utter responsibility of the recipient reader. Under no circumstances will any legal responsibility or blame be held against the publisher for any reparation, damages, or monetary loss due to the information herein, either directly or indirectly.

Respective authors own all copyrights not held by the publisher.

The information herein is offered for informational purposes solely, and is universal as so. The presentation of the information is without contract or any type of guarantee assurance.

The trademarks that are used are without any consent, and the publication of the trademark is without permission or backing by the trademark owner. All trademarks and brands within this book are for clarifying purposes only and are the owned by the owners themselves, not affiliated with this document.

Table of Contents

Introduction ii

Chapter 1:
Success: A Collection of Good Behaviors 7

Chapter 2:
Awareness – An Essential Attitude to Become Successful 13

Chapter #3:
The Complaining Attitude – A Killer of Success 19

Chapter#4:
Attitude Where You Keep Learning – An Essential to
   Stay Successful 24

Chapter #5:
Determination to Not Quit Until You Achieve it 28

Chapter #6:
Taking Massive Action – An Aid to Strong Determination 32

Chapter #7:
Cutting the Bad Influences – An Essential to Succeed 39

Chapter #8:
Hard Work – A Surety to Success 44

Chapter #9:
Taking Responsibility For Your Actions –
   A Must to Succeed 49

Chapter #10:
Delayed Gratification – A Common Trait of the Successful .. 53

Chapter #11:
Sociability – An Attitude All Leaders Must Have 58

Conclusion 63

Before we get to the point of discussing the different behaviors that you need to build to succeed in whichever aspect of life you want to succeed, we will start by understanding the relationship between success and various good behaviors.

Chapter 1:

Success: A Collection of Good Behaviors

A few years ago, I was very concerned about becoming successful in life. At that time, my definition of success was to earn somehow a 6-figure income so that I can enjoy living a quality life wherein I can spend time and money on my friends and family. Also, I wanted to have enough money to travel the world.

Travelling was my passion but I was never able to earn enough in my life to afford a single trip abroad. Instead, my earnings were far too less than an average guy. The reason for that was because I kept on switching jobs every 6 months either of dissatisfaction of the job environment or in most cases, I got fired. I just could not keep a job!

To take care of the expenses, my wife had to work several jobs to meet our financial obligations because I had become far too unreliable at providing for the family. This was quite frustrating for me and it bothered me for a while. As the years passed, the frustration grew to a point wherein I was ready to snap at the slightest sign of provocation even when it was unwarranted. Talking to me became more like walking in a minefield, as I could explode any time.

Then one day, I came across a video on YouTube wherein Warren Buffett was attending a seminar. Somebody asked him in that seminar, *"What is the greatest thing that you feel can keep a person from getting successful?"* He said, *"The threat to success is sloth and unreliability."*

That answer made me think of my behavior towards the jobs I did over the past 5 years. Also, it reminded me of the reasons why I left them. One behavior that was common in all of my previous jobs was my unreliability. Getting late and taking frequent offs was my thing at that time either because I was too lazy to get up early, was unmotivated to go to work because I felt it was paying me too little or I had some other issues at home that I needed to attend. Giving my all to my work was the least of my worries as I felt the bosses were benefiting more from what I was offering than I was benefiting (I developed the attitude that my bosses were using me for their personal gains).

This unreliability factor made me look bad in the eyes of my employers, which often turned back on me in form of bad behavior from my superiors. I got reprimanded often and never appeared in the list of recommendations for promotions and awards. No boss wanted to have me work on something he/she felt needed close attention (even when that meant working overtime) because they knew I would come up with all manner of excuses why the tasks could not be done. At the time, I thought it was good that bosses don't come rushing to me for their rescue when different tasks (especially urgent ones) needed to be done. I felt I had sent the right message that I am not a pushover to all my bosses.

Before I realized that my unreliability was the reason why I was always looking for jobs, I never blamed myself for the ill treatment I got from my superiors. I always thought that they were at fault, which led me to leave the jobs. This behavior realization changed my perspective of success. For the first time, I really started blaming myself for the situation I was in. I thought about how much of a difficult person I had been to my previous bosses, thought about the other employees who were doing all the right things and ended up succeeding by climbing up the corporate ladder of course with all the perks that they were getting. I then took a close look at my life and realized I had been short sighted and not worthy of success based on what I had been doing.

Given that I wasn't sure that I was thinking straight, I decided to change this behavior over the next 6 months to see if the outcome changes or not; I was working at an insurance company. Since, I had decided to do things differently, I worked on my sleeping habits to make sure I never get late for office, made sure nothing side tracked me when I got to work, never took an off (I never got sick) and became more proactive at taking on new projects, working overtime just to complete urgent tasks etc. To my surprise, the regularity and productivity on work really worked for me since the behavior of my superiors really started to change. I felt respected at the job, as there wasn't anyone standing every day to lecture me while entering the office and there were no funny comments from my colleagues and superiors when I was leaving in the evening because I made sure I had my desk cleared up before going home.

For the next six months, I kept following on the same routine and noticed a great performance change at my job. Just after nine months of regularity, productivity and discipline at work, I got my first pay increase. This was a great thing for me, as for the first time in my life, I felt like I am going somewhere at this job.

This small change in my behavior and its effects led me to think differently as I started realizing that success is nothing but a collection of good behaviors. Thereafter, I started studying behaviors of successful people and slowly started adopting them one by one. As a result, my income also got better and better.

After just 6 years, I am earning a 6-figure income, which for me is a huge achievement as I have long surpassed my dream income to earn 100k. The reason I am telling you this is to let you know the importance of good behaviors in your career and life success.

If you ask me now, what is success? My answer is, improving oneself on daily basis. When I say improvement, I mean identifying bad behaviors that can stop you from growing and working on them on daily basis to make sure you keep going forward whether it's moving forward in your career or your life goals.

In the coming chapters, I am going to discuss some very important behaviors that are essential for success, whether it's in your career or life. Also, we will discuss how you can adopt these essential behaviors of success, so you never fall back on your career and life goals.

From the above discussion, I'd like to quote some inspiring quotes to get you thinking:

- *"Successful people form the habit of doing what failures won't do."*
- *"Successful people are just those with successful habits"* Bryan Tracy
- *"You must master your habits or they will master you"*

- *"We are what we repeatedly do. Excellence, then, is not an act, but a habit."* Will Durant

When you think closely, you will realize that the habits that all the quotes above refer to are just behaviors. As such, for our case in this book, we can create our new set of quotes:

- *"Successful people form the behavior of doing what failures won't do."*

- *"Successful people are just those with successful behaviors"*

- *"You must master your behaviors or they will master you"*

- *"We are what we repeatedly do. Excellence, then, is not an act, but a behavior."*

That's why this book focuses primarily on helping you to avoid behaviors, which you should avoid (because they pull you away from success and closer to failure) and those you should embrace (because they pull you towards success and away from failure) if you are to become the success that you desperately want to become.

The first behavior that we will talk about is awareness, as it forms the foundation of all the other behaviors that you need to work on. Let's discuss that next.

Chapter 2:

Awareness – An Essential Attitude to Become Successful

One thing that can totally ruin your success is your ignorant attitude towards life. I know it's very difficult to live in the present. However, the fact you need to realize is; you will not go anywhere if you keep thinking of the past or future.

Why is that?

Well, if you are fixated on the past or the future, you lose the opportunities that are right in front of you because you will not be able to see them. Also, you will not recognize what behaviors of yours are making you fail and restricting you from living a successful, fulfilling life.

Since, I had been a victim of this attitude for so many years, you should learn from my mistakes. I was an ignorant person that used to live either in the past or the future. I was always thinking that the next boss will be more understanding, the next job will be more flexible etc. I was also thinking of going home the moment I walked into the office, partly because my superiors and colleagues seemed to have this mean look whenever I walked in late either in the morning or after lunch. I also was stuck in my past of how bad bosses can be, how I got fired, how unappreciative my previous boss was (so I thought this new one would not be any better), how hard my job was etc. Unfortunately, this only took me away from what was actually important; my present job/task, as they clouded my judgment and made me have a bad attitude.

Well, as you are aware by now, the cost of not living in the present was huge. My relationship was suffering and so did my health. However, the most affected part of my life was my financial situation. This was all happening because I wasn't aware of my behaviors that were restricting me from achieving my life goals.

Luckily, it all changed the day when I first realized about my unreliable behavior and the way it was affecting my financial success. If I kept on doing things the old way, without being aware of my behaviors, I would have never achieved the success I have right now. That's why I feel it should be a part of this book since it is about getting successful, which is never going to happen if you have an ignorant attitude towards different facets of your life that need to be changed for you to realize success in those areas. Think about it; if you have an ignorant attitude, you cannot realize the behaviors that you have, which are making you have a hard time attaining your dreams.

After realizing the importance of awareness, I listened to many successful people to know which behaviors were essential to get successful in life. I kept myself under analysis all the time to know whether those behaviors were a part of me or not. Furthermore, I trained my mind to stay present all the time to make sure that I don't lose the opportunity that is right in front of me. I should tell you this; training myself to live in the present, being aware of my own behaviors and how they were keeping me from reaching my goals was hardest challenge of my life.

It was challenging for me. That's why, I am sure, it will also be challenging for you.

Why is that, you may ask?

Well, it is challenging because our minds have gotten used to running on autopilot 24/7. We are just used to thinking in a certain way because of the beliefs we have built over time regarding different issues. You will find yourself going back to your old ways of thinking without even actually being actively aware about it. If procrastination has been your default way of life, you may still find it hard to stop giving excuses why you cannot get stuff done on time. That's where you need awareness to 'catch' yourself when doing it so that you can call yourself out, challenge these tendencies and get more done.

Let me show you how I trained myself to let go of my ignorant attitude in order to stay aware and live in the present. Here are the steps I took to change myself to stay aware all the time. You can do the same to get your desired results.

Step 1: I realized that my inner voices were the reasons that kept me from staying in the present. Whenever some thought came into my head, either from the past or the future, I snubbed it by repeating an affirmation or any statement that I knew was true. Also, I tried to focus on something in the present.

Let me clarify that by an example. Whenever, a thought came in my head from an incident that happened in the past or some worry regarding the future, I repeated this affirmation, *"It is necessary for me to focus on the present."* I used to keep repeating this statement until the voices in my head were gone. Also, whenever I 'caught myself' thinking that my employer was benefiting more than I do in the work relationship, I simply told myself off with a statement like: *"That is not true; look at all the other people who have build a career out of what I am doing. I am not the special one. And in any case, the money I make here is making a difference in my family's life. Work is a mutually beneficial relationship- the employer has to make a profit by keeping me here. I would do the same when I am an employer".*

When that used to happen, I immediately used to bring my focus on something in my environment. I kept on doing this for about 6 months until the voices in my head stopped bothering me. After 6 months of struggle, I felt a big change in my attitude, as I felt the way I viewed my environment was far much better than it used to be. This helped a lot in showing me the opportunities that I could take advantage of right away.

Step 2: I also started to notice some of my bad behaviors and their repercussions, which motivated me to change them so I could get my desired result. I did that by noticing the effects of a behavior, which gave me a reason to change it.

All this only got possible, as I got better at staying aware all the time. That's why you should work on staying aware as well if you really want to notice the effects of behaviors that are making you not get far in life as far as attaining your dreams is concerned. It is only when you are aware of the present that you will notice the success-sabotaging behaviors that you have and their effects. Only then can you take the necessary steps (being fully aware of the effects that they are having on your life) to change your life for the better.

When you've worked on your awareness of the present (this is something you will be doing all the time), now you can start working on fixing some of the success sabotaging behaviors and transforming your life with desirable behaviors.

Chapter #3:

The Complaining Attitude – A Killer of Success

Once I got to know the importance of behaviors in living a successful life, I started studying a lot of successful people and tried to find the factors that made them successful. I found out a common behavior of successful people that was missing in me which was that they were not complainers like me.

I realized that this attitude needed to change if I was to unlock success and keep on succeeding. My complaining attitude came out as always having explanations why I was failing and others were succeeding. It was just never my fault. This was something that was keeping me from getting my life goals because whenever I heard a success story, I used to say, "*He had that advantage, which I didn't have, blah! blah! blah!*"

Once I realized the complaining attitude was just an excuse to not get bothered by my failures, I knew I had to change it. But, how? That was a difficult question for me at that time since I had decided to change it but didn't know how I was going to do that. I simply kept saying to myself, "*I know, I have all the necessary tools to get successful."* I was repeating this affirmation since I didn't know any other way. Also, this was because of the fact that the affirmation worked for me while I was training myself to stay aware.

To my surprise, it did raise my self-belief but I was still struggling to get over my complaining attitude.

I knew, I had to find some other way. I felt I needed to change some of my ideologies about success. However, I didn't know which ideologies needed the change. Since I had already indulged myself into reading about successful people, to my aid came a book by Grant Cardone whose title was, *"Be Obsessed or Be Average"*. This book changed all my ideologies about success. By reading his story, I came to know what success really is. If you don't know his story, let me summarize it for you. He was a drug addict at the age of 26 and was working as a car salesman. According to him, he hated his job and wasn't a good salesman but being tired of his poor lifestyle and the fact that he didn't have any other option, he decided to get good at sales even though he hated it. After reading many sales books and trying countless sales strategies, he got so good in sales that now he is one of the best sales trainers in the world. He now works with companies such as Google and Amazon and has a net worth around $500 million.

This was a massive reveal for me since before that, I used to think that someone can only be successful in something that he/she is naturally good at or he/she enjoys doing it. However, after reading his story, I got my answer. I knew that I don't have to feel good doing something to get successful. I just need to do it enough times to get good at it. The answer to success was not something you enjoy doing; rather, it was just doing an activity again and again and keeping learning from your mistakes to get better at it. This was something that I later observed in the life stories of every successful person I read. I even discovered Winston Churchill's quote on success and failures:

"Success is the ability to go from failure to failure without losing your enthusiasm."

From then on, I started to think differently and I encourage you to do the same too. If you want to live a successful life:

- Don't think you can get successful overnight. The main reason you complain about other people's achievements is because you think that they have somehow got successful overnight or that they were lucky. However, upon careful reflection, I realized that there is no such thing as luck. It's all about working hard to develop a specific skill. When you think someone is an overnight success, look keenly in his/her life. You will realize that he/she has perhaps failed countless times. Steve Jobs' quote aptly describes this:

"If you really look closely, most overnight successes took a long time."

Let me also add Mark Cuban's quote:

"It doesn't matter how many times you fail. You only have to be right once and then everyone can tell you that you are an overnight success."

What I mean here is that you can be successful in anything you choose to put your focus on and have decided to get better at it each day.

- Don't waste your time trying to find your passion. The statement that we all hear that we should 'follow our passion' is good but that does not mean you should sit around for months or years trying to figure out you're your elusive passion is. The attitude you need to develop is to "just do it" and stop whining. Whatever you have in front of you, do it then get better at it. Don't be afraid of failing and remember; failing is just a part of learning process. If you keep quitting things just because you failed at something or you don't like doing it, then you will keep on changing careers and other goals in life. Also, you can't be good at anything if you keep dabbling and trying all manner of things hoping to strike overnight success on something you don't know much about.

- Remember to take massive action. Failing sometimes creates a doubt in your mind that keeps you from taking action. Unfortunately, if you stop taking action, you will never achieve anything in life. I can always recall the success story of Thomas Edison's invention of the light bulb that he invented after a 1000 failures. If he would have stopped only at first or second failure then the history books wouldn't have Thomas Edison in them.

These ideologies made my complaining attitude to go away. If you do have the same attitude, work towards changing your attitude because if you don't, you will keep complaining your whole life and never get anywhere.

Chapter #4:

Attitude Where You Keep Learning – An Essential to Stay Successful

You may have noticed that some people always stay successful while others get success for a short period and then they go back to their old circumstances.

Have you ever wondered why this happens? Why do some people seem to be always good at making money or living in a happy relationship or keeping themselves in their desired shape? Why don't you keep making money the way someone else does? Why is your paycheck stuck at a certain level while your colleagues keep on increasing theirs often?

I know, it bothered me too when I was working at the insurance company. I wondered why my colleagues were getting higher and higher paychecks every month while I was stuck on producing the same income. At that time, I didn't realize the importance of having the attitude to keep learning, which is essential to stay successful. It first came to my attention when my boss kept asking me of the discussions I had with the prospects I met, each day. I wondered why he did that. At first, I thought, he may like to interfere to show me that he is the boss. However, this changed the day when I was finding difficulty in closing an insurance deal. I thought to take my boss with me, to show him, how difficult it was to close a deal so he doesn't pressurize me again when I fall short on my targets. To my surprise, he closed it so easily that I felt ashamed of myself for taking him.

On the way back, I asked him how he was able to close that deal so easily since he had not been into sales for the last three years. His response was, *"I may have left going in the field but I get more experience now than I could ever get in the field because now I have the power of reaching 10 customers at a time rather than reaching one that I used to when I was doing sales myself."* I asked him, what he meant by reaching 10 customers at a time. He said, *"Now I have a team of 10 whom I listen to each day. This way, I get to learn more each day than I was learning when I was doing sales myself.*

I asked him: why do you need to learn now; you don't have to do sales anymore? His response was, *"I earn 3 times more than you now. If somehow life throws me back into a situation wherein I have to do sales again, this experience will ensure that I keep earning the same amount regardless of my position."*

By listening to his response, I realized the importance of having an attitude of learning all the time. I got my answer of why the rich stay rich and even get richer. The answer was simple; they ensure that they keep on learning so they don't get ruled by the circumstances they are in. They don't let events in their lives affect their success since they are improving at what they do each day. Therefore, if life throws them something unexpected, they are ready for it more than others which make them stay ahead of the game. I took this experience very seriously and decided to develop the attitude of always learning.

Here is how I ensured that I keep on learning new approaches of doing things so that I could never be broke again. To ensure that I have the attitude to keep learning, I trained my mind not to feel comfortable since doing that means I am not learning anything new. I did that by challenging my inner voice since that's the voice that told me whether I was in my comfort zone or not. So whenever a thought popped up in my head telling me that I have done enough for the day, I challenged it by doing the opposite action. This way, I ensured I stay away from my comfort zone by stretching myself physically and mentally. And in the process, I realized that I could take much more than I ever thought was possible. I made sure I learned something new or perfected my craft of doing something that I was already good at every day and this pushed me to a point where I became exceptionally good at such that I was requested to guide my colleagues whenever they needed help.

You can follow the same trick. Let me give you an example on how to do that. Let's say you are cold calling someone to get leads. You have already done 50 calls and then a voice in your head says, *"Ok! I think I have done enough for today."*

Here is what to do:

Don't let that thought rule you. Instantly pick up the phone and do a few more calls. Do this every time you hear that inner voice because that is your comfort zone. Keep pushing it every day for the next 3 – 6 months. By doing this, you will develop a habit of staying out of your comfort zone, which will ensure that you stay hungry to learn.

Chapter #5:

Determination to Not Quit Until You Achieve it

One thing that sets apart any successful person from those who haven't achieved what they desired is their strong determination. When you look around you closely, you will realize that all the successful people have this frame of mind to not quit until they achieve what they desire. Do you think Elon Musk could build the first private space shuttle if he gave up or thought this was only stuff that NASA and other government funded bodies could do? Do you think Thomas Edison would try so many times to make a light bulb? Do you think Michael Jordan would become what he became without determination? You can bet he wouldn't.

Strong determination pushes successful people to keep moving closer to their goals, as they keep learning from their mistakes and try a different approach to do things to avoid the previous mistake from happening. Let me quote Michael Jordan to explain this point:

"I've missed more than 9000 shots in my career. I've lost almost 300 games. 26 times, I've been trusted to take the game winning shot and missed. I've failed over and over and over again in my life. And that is why I succeed."

In simpler terms, when he failed, he went back to training until he had transformed that weakness to a strength. You can see this attitude in any successful person you encounter or read regardless of his/her profession and his/her definition of success. If you ever want to have a successful career or want to live a successful life, you have to be so determined that you will not quit until you achieve it.

It's easy to say but very hard to do. However, the fact is; you won't ever get successful at anything without a strong determination. So how can you ensure that you never quit until you achieve your goals? For that, you have to change some of your ideologies. I did that 5 years ago when I was still working for the insurance company. Here is how I started to think and I encourage you do the same if you want to succeed at anything.

1: Don't be afraid of making mistakes

Mistakes are a part of learning process; I can't avoid them so I should not be afraid of making them. This is because making mistakes will only tell me what not to do next time hence they will only make me a better person. Thomas Edison discovered 1000 ways of how not to make a light bulb before he finally made one.

This ideology is great but when it came to putting it into practice, I was still afraid of making mistakes.

However, I did trick myself by saying that if Thomas Edison tried 1000 times before he found out how to make a light bulb, then I have no reason to quit after a few tries. I put my limit for the number of failed attempts at 1000 before I could start giving myself excuses why something cannot be done. Well, I wasn't trying to reinvent the wheel or light bulb; I simply wanted to make more money (six figure income) to support my family and still have lots of money left for everything I wanted to do, which included traveling. The truth is; I wasn't sure I would be able to do that even after a thousand failures, but I committed myself to try it.

I started carrying a pen and notepad with me all the time. Whenever I failed to close a client, I wrote the discussion on the notepad. Later on, when I used to come home from the job, I used to read all the discussions I had and identify the mistake(s) I did. I gave each mistake a number. I kept on doing that for 4 months and had 7 notepads filled with discussions and mistakes. To my amazement, I hadn't reached half way to the 1000 mistake mark and I was already closing twice the number of deals than I used to close 4 months earlier.

This raised my belief in; *"mistakes are part of the learning process"* ideology and as the time passed, I got less and less afraid of making mistakes because I knew that if I make a mistake, I would not make such a mistake next time because I would have prepared myself adequately to ensure I don't make that mistake. After 6 months of following the same routine; noting mistakes, avoiding the same action to observe difference in results and then finally achieving what I desired, my ideology was totally changed from being afraid of making mistakes to not being afraid of mistakes.

I encourage you do the same if you want to have a strong determination and want to believe that mistakes are only part of your success journey.

Chapter #6:

Taking Massive Action – An Aid to Strong Determination

As I discussed in previous chapter, determination is one key element that separates a successful person from an unsuccessful one. Without determination, you cannot get even close to being a success irrespective of what your definition of success is. The question however is; what if you still lose your determination despite giving it your all? What do you rely on to get ahead in life? Well, to understand that, you need to know how your mind works.

When you set your success goals, you set a time frame to achieve them. When you don't achieve them on time, you lose your determination whether or not your ideology about success is correct. Your belief in your ability to get stuff done, according to plan, fades as the number of failures keeps increasing. It can get to a desperate situation where you now throw the towel and give up if success does not seem forthcoming even after multiple tries. The question is; how can you ensure that you never lose determination and achieve your goals on time?

For that to happen, you need to take massive action towards your goals, as this will make your learning process faster than the average guy. And as you learn faster, you achieve your goals faster. I am not saying that you will always achieve your goals on time; at least not in the start but soon, you will notice that you are accomplishing much more than you ever did. They say the secret to getting ahead in life is getting started. I can take it a little further and say that the secret to standing out is taking massive action because if you don't, you can bet that you won't make any visible progress. You can't expect to be any different if you are doing the same things that you've always done. When you take massive action and succeed multiple times, you start getting addicted to success because of the satisfaction that comes with succeeding in whatever you do. This in turn also boosts your determination because you will always know that you are capable of doing anything you set your mind on irrespective of how long it takes.

I have been a victim of losing my determination even though I was not afraid of making mistakes. It happened to me when I started my first online business 4 years ago at a time when I was looking to add another income stream besides doing insurance sales. In those days, Tee Spring was a huge hit. There were many success stories of people making millions in just a year. I was fascinated too of building my own business but I wasn't ready to quit my job before I ensure that I can survive without it. I set a goal to earn at least $10,000 in the first 3 months in T-shirt sales. My goal wasn't really high as I only had 4 hours to spend each day with other things going on in my life. So, I designed some T shirts and let everyone in my social circle know I was doing this. I had the strategy in place that I worked on for the next 3 months. After 3 months of spending time and money, I wasn't able to achieve my desired outcome of generating $10,000 in profit, which in turn made me lose my motivation. When I finally got fed up of business, I sat down and thought of the mistakes I made in the first 3 months. To my surprise, there wasn't any as I was doing everything according to plan. However, what lacked in my plan was taking massive action to ensure that I achieve my desired outcome on time. I was only doing activities that an average person without much of a plan can do in that time but my goal for first 3 months wasn't average for just a startup business. Upon this realization, I decided to give this another try for the next three months with a revised plan. The only difference in my plan was doing the same activity 3 - 4 times faster than I used to, so I can do more in less time. I was ready to take massive action and didn't care about the results. After three months of taking massive action, I was able to produce a net profit of $6,340 by doing the same actions but doing them a little faster. I felt very determined to go to the next level and my motivation was on the roof. It was then that I figured out the importance of taking massive action. Don't just do the bare minimum if you want to stand out from the rest.

Strive to do what others only dream of doing and you will get the results that people dream of getting.

Here is how you can develop a habit of taking massive action to ensure you reach your goals on time and in turn keep your determination high.

- **Time every action:** It is simple yet challenging. Whenever you are making a strategy to achieve your goals, make sure you set a time for each action you have to take to achieve those goals. Do this not only for monthly but also for daily goals. For example, if you are in an online business wherein your monthly goal is to increase your social presence, you can plan to do 300 tweets in a month or an average of 10 tweets a day. Don't just say you will tweet 10 times daily; set the time you will do that and how long you will spend on Twitter.

- **Challenge your mind:** When you set the time for each action, don't set the time that your mind tells you; rather, set half of that time. In the above example, if you have to do 10 tweets a day, your mind might tell you that you need 30 minutes per day. Instead of going for 30 minutes, go for 15 minutes. There is a saying that work expands and contracts to fit the available time for its completion. This is to say that if you allocate less time, you will still get the job done. Therefore, if you dedicate 15 minutes for the tweets, you will still find yourself doing all the stuff you would otherwise have done in 30 minutes!

- **Don't get discouraged:** When you set half the time for the activities you have planned for the day, you might not be able to do that activity in that specific time on the first day. However, don't get discouraged. Rather, keep pushing your mind on daily basis to ensure you are not doing what the average guy is doing; you need to be different! Keep doing it for a week or two and you will start doing the activities within your set time. Once that happens, again challenge your brain by setting half the time for the same activity. This way, you will ensure that you keep pushing your boundaries. In the process, you will develop the habit of taking massive action. Highly productive and successful people don't just wing it in life; they plan their time meticulously because they understand every minute counts. And not doing one activity promptly might mean that everything else for the rest of the day or week for instance ends up getting delayed. They cannot afford that and you too need to have that mindset. Think of yourself as a CEO of your own imaginary enterprise with meetings upon meetings coupled with a few minutes or hours of deskwork. Do you think you can afford to chat your friends on Facebook and share memes on WhatsApp when your tray is full yet you have another meeting to attend or somewhere you have to rush to in 1 hour? You definitely wouldn't. Start feeling that your time is occupied (having to do lists can help you to create that feeling so that you don't develop the feeling that 'there is a lot of time left') and you will undoubtedly notice a significant change in the way you spend your time.

Taking massive action will set you apart from everyone around you. When you are not taking average action, you can't expect average results! Massive action will bring massive results so keep pushing yourself by biting as much as you can chew (don't leave so much space)! Think of when babies are trying to walk or talk; they don't care about the number of times they make mistakes. Sometimes these mistakes mean getting hurt when trying to walk for instance. If babies don't take massive action to start walking (which is really a risky adventure since they don't have balance yet), they can't ever start walking well. The same applies to every facet of your life; if you want big results, take big steps to success.

As you do that, you ought to keep off bad influence.

Chapter #7:

Cutting the Bad Influences – An Essential to Succeed

Another very important behavior of successful people is that they stay away from the wrong people or environment. They try to associate themselves with like-minded people and cut negative minded people from their lives. If you look around keenly, you won't see any successful person spending too much time with whiners, people who don't have anything good to say about life, people who don't take action to make positive progress in their life etc.

I know you might be wondering; so what's wrong with spending time with anyone, whether positive or negative?

Well, negative people are like energy suckers/leeches; they just suck out all the positivity, motivation and determination in you to a point where you can't get much done. Negativity is contagious (especially given that we have a negativity bias- we listen to and believe the negative more than the positive). As such, no matter how positive you are, if you have negative people around you, you will have a hard time making real progress. In fact, you may soon find yourself going back to the habit of complaining if you have complainers around you.

I was a victim of this behavior 3 years ago when I was running an online T-shirt business. At that time, I used to sit with my old buddies from the job. I was earning close to 6-figure income, which was well ahead of the expectations of people I spend time with. The guys always said that this business sounded too good to be true. They just wondered how I could make money developing t-shirt designs (not even making the t-shirts themselves). They then talked about how they had heard other people had their businesses crash after making thousands of dollars a month, as I was doing. While I was constantly telling them off, soon, the idea that the business could crash soon started downing on me. I then became less aggressive, lazier and didn't take as much action as I used to. And before I could realize it, the sales of my business started to decline. As I started discussing it with my old colleagues, I heard answers such as; it's happening to everybody these days because the economy is down or there is too much competition nowadays; that's why your business is on a decline. Some were even saying such things like "I told you"!

My belief in what others were saying about the business became stronger especially whenever my t-shirts sales made a new low; I gave the same reasons to myself. As a result, after just 8 months of constant drop in sales, my profit declined from $8,500 per month to less than $3000 a month. It was the time I started feeling worried because now I was earning less than what I used to at my job.

I started seeking help from someone who was earning more than me in the same business. To my rescue, I came across a program of some guy on the internet. The program was about how to make your first million through T-shirt sales; the author of the program had recently made his first million in the same industry. I was amazed to see the achievement that this guy had as I was struggling to make a consistent 6 figure income at that time. I enrolled to the program and saw all the things he did to earn a 7 figure income. As part of the program, he was also personally mentoring the first 100 candidates of which I was also one. In his mentorship, we came close to each other. We lived in the same city so we also started hanging out a little. I was impressed by his ideologies of business as it was totally the opposite of my ideologies or you can say my colleagues' ideologies, which they transferred to me.

He never complaint about the economy being bad, he thought of competition as a friend to learn what to do and what not to do. After just spending 6 months with him, I was able to generate a $30,000 profit in a month. After some time, I also started having the same ideologies about the competition and the economy. At that time, I realized the importance of having good company since I wasn't meeting much of my old colleagues in that 6 months period. I decided to totally cut off people that had a bad influence in my life and meet positive people who can drive me forward. I did that for the next 2 years wherein I totally stopped meeting my old colleagues and chose to stay around positive, successful people. As a result, after just 2 years, I was earning close to 7-figure income that was totally beyond what I expected of myself.

The reason I am telling you this so you can learn from my mistake too. Stop spending time with people that have in any way a bad influence on you, as they will influence you negatively whether you want to accept it or not. So how do you go about it?

Here are some ideas:

- Avoid calling or answering calls from people who always have something to complain about. They don't have any achievement of their own and try to bad mouth others who have achieved something in life. What you need to realize is that such people do that because they are jealous of other people's achievements.

- Stop going to places where you will meet your old friends especially if they haven't achieved anything in life themselves. This will ensure that you don't have to meet them.

- Start visiting places where you will find successful people who are oozing with positivity. They are not in the pubs wasting their time and money; rather, you can find them in business conventions or charity events.

- Minimize your exposure to social media, news and other information sources. When you look keenly, you will realize that a big percentage of what you see on social media and in news is negative; it could be how the president is ruining this country, how a war is about to happen, how the politicians are stealing public resources etc. All these things will just work you up for no good reason and may only end up making you to not put your all in getting stuff done.

Do all the things mentioned above to ensure that you cut off all the bad influence in your life and meet positive, successful people. This way, you will soon start to think and act like them, something that will undoubtedly propel you to success and sustain you in your quest to success.

Chapter #8:

Hard Work – A Surety to Success

There is a saying that goes; "the harder you work, the luckier you get". However, I wouldn't really think of the luck the same way you think of winning a lottery. I think of it as increasing your capacity to spot opportunities and take them before anyone else does. This perhaps explains why another quote says: "Luck is what happens when preparation meets opportunity". Thomas Jefferson even went on to say, "*I am a great believer in luck, and I find the harder I work, the more I have of it.*"

All this is true; if you ever want to be successful in life, you can never neglect the importance of hard work. In fact, you won't see any successful person say that hard work is not necessary to succeed. Only lazy people think the secret to success is working smart! You can't work smart if you don't know how to work hard! You work hard then devise means to become smart in your work so that you can get more done more efficiently.

However, if you have heard someone saying that smart work is more important than hard work, then you might not have understood him/her correctly.

What that person meant by saying 'smart work' is doing the hard work combined with awareness to change your outcome. This definition of hard work is really important for you to understand because many people say that they are doing the hard work yet they don't succeed in life because their definition of hard work is wrong. If the definition of hard work was just laboring 12-14 hours a day without thinking of the outcome and trying something different to change it then your school's janitor would be the most successful person in the world because according to this definition, he works hard. However, you don't see janitors who are millionaires or billionaires. This means there is something missing in this definition of hard work. The true definition of hard work is, to do a certain task with an outcome in mind; keep a check on the results of your actions and improvise to get your desired results.

By working hard this way, you make sure that you don't move away from your goals in life.

I also had a wrong definition of hard work at one stage in my life when I was working on an 8 hours shift at KFC and babysitting my neighbor's kids for 6 hours a day. I thought I was doing all the hard work I need to succeed but the reality was; I was doing labor. After doing both jobs for more than a year, I observed I wasn't going anywhere in life and then I got fired from my KFC job because of my regularity issue. After that,

I was hired by the insurance company in a target based sales job. That was the first time in my life I understood the true definition of hard work because before that, all my jobs were not target oriented. In all my previous jobs, I didn't have to achieve a certain target to get my pay, which made me do things like others were already doing. While doing these jobs, I never thought of improving my actions to change the outcome in my favor. In any case, the pay was guaranteed at the end of the day (all I needed was to clock in when my shift started and clock out when my shift ended). I never cared to understand what my input to the companies was worth; I just had this idea that the companies are benefiting too much from me. Well, that was until I landed in a sales job that clearly had me understand what I was bringing to the company. I realized it was very minimal! That's why I feel a target oriented job is the best when it comes to self improvement and understanding the true definitions of hard work.

Here is how you can train yourself to work hard to make sure that you achieve your life and career goals.

- Set a target for yourself and set a time limit to achieve that target. For example, if you want to live a rich lifestyle, set an income you desire to earn to live that lifestyle. Also, set the date you want it to be achieved.

- Decide what sort of career you want to get into and have a clear strategy on how to grow in that profession.

- Notice what actions are taking you towards your goals and what actions are making you stay behind on your dreams. For that, you need to be aware all the time. I have discussed that part previously in this book so I won't get into details.

- Keep improvising and revising your strategy since there is no way you will have a perfect strategy. You will make mistakes along the way; accept that fact and don't be afraid of making them. Use these as learning experiences to know one way of not accomplishing whatever goals you have.

- Keep challenging yourself to achieve the next level. You can do that by leaving your comfort zone. I have also covered that part in the book so won't get into that as well.

- Ensure to put in the hours required to achieve your goals. Without putting effort in executing a particular action, you will not get good at it. For instance, if you are in a sales job, you need to interact with more and more people on daily. Do it more than your job requires you to do. If it requires you to meet 10 prospects a day, then go meet 15. This will help ensure that you become great at meeting people.

Do all the steps mentioned above to ensure you train yourself for real hard work, as this is the only way to live a successful life.

Chapter #9:

Taking Responsibility For Your Actions – A Must to Succeed

Another very important behavior that you will find common in successful people is that they are accountable of their own actions and don't blame others or their environment for their failures. They understand that they have chosen a certain path for themselves and they can fail along the way. They don't find people to blame for their own failures; rather, they learn from their failures and don't forget to take a different approach in the next try.

Accountability is a very important trait you should have in your personality since it is the only way you can grow. If you start blaming others for your failures, you will never learn from your mistakes since you don't see yourself as the one at fault. Also, you will feel hatred towards that person who you think is the reason for your failure, which will affect your productivity and overall mental health.

I have been through this when I started my first online T-shirt selling business 4 years ago. I chose that business for a reason. I was doing the sales job those days and wanted to have my own business. I didn't have a lot of money to spend on an offline business. I also didn't have the energy to go out again after getting back from work. Therefore, I decided to look for opportunities to earn online and I came across a YouTube video of a person who started this T-shirt selling business 3 months before with just $200 and made a profit of $1,500 in just 3 months. He was selling a course on how he did that. I bought his $100-course and did exactly the same stuff.

After 3 months, I was able to generate only 2 sales accumulating $40 dollars in profit. Since I had spent $100 on the course, that meant I was still at a loss of $60. I had already spent so many hours getting the sales so I really felt frustrated that the course did not generate the promised return. I started blaming that guy rather than taking the accountability for my own failure. I used to think that he scammed me so I hated the guy. The hatred was so intense that I forgot to look into this experience any other way. One of my high school friends came to visit me those days. I told him the whole story of how I got scammed by someone online. His response came as a shock to me when he mentioned that he also purchased the same course a month earlier and his first month sales made him $800 in profit. His story made my hatred to go away since I couldn't blame my failures on that guy anymore, as I had proof that his strategy was working. Later that night, when I was on my bed, I revisited the events of my past and thought why I chose that business model.

It was clear; I only had limited time and money. Then I asked myself this next question; "If I chose this business for myself, why I was blaming someone else for my failure." Deep down, I knew the answer but I was afraid to admit it. I just wanted to say that I tried but it didn't work out. I didn't want to put the blame on myself so I put it on someone else because it was easy.

After the self-talk, I was a bit relieved as now I had confessed to myself that I was afraid of failing and was looking for someone to blame for it. The next morning, I woke up satisfied. I knew what I had to do. I had to look for the mistakes I made and the way I can avoid those next time. I wasn't able to do that before because I wasn't taking responsibility for my own actions. After that incident, I never looked back on that business and kept on growing except for a few hitches along the way that I had discussed earlier in this book. You can also learn a lesson from my experience and take responsibility for your own actions, which will ensure that you look for the reasons of your failure and try to work on them to get your desired result.

Here is how you can train yourself to be accountable for your actions.

- Think of why are engaging in a particular action and never forget it. In my case, I chose that business because I was limited by time and the amount of money I had.

- Don't expect someone else to come to your rescue. Take someone's experience and make your own path with it. I was expecting that program to be my rescue and hence I copied him from A –Z rather than using my mind to tweak it to my benefit. I didn't think of what I could take from that guy's experience and implement it my own way which was the reason I started blaming him as soon as I failed.

- If you fail using your own mind then take accountability of it. You can do that by accepting the failure and looking for the mistakes you made that you can avoid next time. Also, you can recall why you chose to do something you did.

The more you develop the mindset and behavior to take responsibility for your actions and inactions, the more you will take actions that will propel you to the success you are looking for. This is because you know that success or failure is all in your hands.

Chapter #10:

Delayed Gratification – A Common Trait of the Successful

Another very common behavior that separates the successful from unsuccessful people is their ability to control themselves and understand the importance of delayed gratification. When you are addicted to instant gratification, your mind tells you to not to do things that are necessary to do right now; rather, it tells you to enjoy the present moment as you can always do those things in the future. But as you are well aware, this future time never comes. Instead, you always seem to be having immediate gratifications that you should meet. With such a behavior, you really cannot make any real progress in life.

You may have noticed how the behavior of enjoying instant gratifications is so hard to overcome when trying to lose weight, trying to avoid your unnecessary shopping habit that is making it hard to save enough and invest, when trying to get rid of your procrastination habit and in any other situation. Awareness is the first step to overcoming this bad behavior. You may have noticed something like this; whenever you want to eat something that you know will make you to put on weight, your mind tells you that it's ok to eat it right now, as you can always start the diet tomorrow. Same thing happens when you try to avoid going on a shopping spree, your mind tells you that you can save from the next month. You may have doing such things your whole life and that is why you are not where you expect yourself to be.

I was also an addict of instant gratification when I was switching jobs and was trying to find out the perfect job for myself that could give me all I wanted at that time. However, this all changed when I started to work on my regularity issue on my first successful job that was of insurance sales. When I realized that the misbehavior of my superiors was because of my irregular show ups at work, I tried to change it by going to work on time every day. It was not easy for me at that point since waking up early every day was not my thing. I had the alarm clock before as well but I never woke up on the sound of that alarm. In fact, the first month after having this realization was the toughest of my life. Whenever that alarm went off in the morning, I used to get conscious and think if I can just go to sleep for another 5 minutes. However, I never used to wake up after 5 minutes; I woke up close to an hour later. And for sure, those were the days when I got scolded for getting late without an explanation.

As the days went by, it became harder and harder for me to bear my boss' scolding, which made me readjust my thinking process. After a month of constant scolding from my boss, I felt very angry at myself but not at my boss this time since I now knew it was not his fault but mine. This made my resolve to go to work on time stronger than ever. This time, whenever that alarm went off at 5AM in the morning, I used to get conscious and think what it will cost me if I didn't get out my bed immediately and used to imagine my boss' face as I enter the office. This made me get so uncomfortable that I woke up instantly without telling myself that I could go to sleep for another 5 minutes. As I started going to work on time, my boss and colleagues started treating me differently and I started feeling good about going to work. I was not the same person that I used to be. I was not a slave of the instant gratification of sleeping for '5 more minutes' anymore and this changed my life. It will also change yours if you too train yourself to enjoy delayed gratification.

Here is how you can train yourself to enjoy delayed gratification.

- Try to feel the miserable situation that you are in right now and associate it with your actions. For example, if you are obese then try to feel the miserable life you have because of obesity; you can't wear clothes of your choice and you can't date women that your desire. Now start telling yourself that you are obese because you eat ice cream, chocolate, processed foods and all manner of junk all the time.

- Think of the results of your actions if you don't take the right action now. Try to visualize the outcome as if it is happening right now in front of you. For example, if you are trying to get rid of your procrastination habit, which is making you not to take action, then think of the outcome of your procrastination; visualize yourself living the miserable life. Think of you growing old without having built enough savings for retirement, you being sick in old age because of your current actions, you dying younger because of your eating habits etc. The clearer the image, the more it will make you do things in the present that you don't like to do.

- Motivate yourself to take the action right now. You can do that by following the above two steps; feeling the miserable now and thinking of the future outcome if you don't take the action now.

- Once you start taking action, notice how it changes your future and enjoy the outcome. For example, assume you stopped yourself from going on a shopping spree by following the instructions above. Now observe that at the end of the month, you have an extra $1000 to invest somewhere. Invest it and enjoy the reward even if it's just making you $20 per month. Remember; you don't have to work for those $20!

By following the above guidelines, you will train yourself for delayed gratification. Once that happens, there is no stopping you from achieving your career and life goals.

Chapter #11:

Sociability – An Attitude All Leaders Must Have

Sociability is common trait you see in all the successful leaders of this world. Have you ever thought why? If you haven't, then let me explain why the successful tend to be so social irrespective of their personality traits:

People make up the world we live in. For us to succeed in it, we need connections. To make connections, we have to surround ourselves with positive and powerful people. However, just surrounding yourself with such people doesn't ensure that you will make connections with them. However, if you have a friendly personality and are easy to talk to, then you can be sure to make those connections.

The question is; how can a person be friendly? Isn't that a trait that someone is gifted with naturally? No, it's not. In fact, I thought like that too for a while until I met a guy at a high school reunion. He was my classmate until 9th grade then he left school because his parents were shifting to another town. The way I remembered this guy was totally different than the way I saw at the reunion. At high school, he used to be a loner, not talking to anybody, sitting at the corner of our class doing his own thing. However, he wasn't that guy anymore. I remember when I saw him at the reunion, he was surrounded by 7 people and all were laughing at his jokes.

I was in shock to see that guy this way. I never imagined him to be like that. Then, I observed two of my high school buddies were also in that group. I went there to meet them and greeted that guy in courtesy. I stood there for a while expecting my friends to move along with me but as the time passed, none of us moved. This guy who was once a loner has now completely transformed into a very jolly fellow. He was too friendly to talk to and has amazing stories to share with us. We stood there for half an hour with him. After that, I felt like he was one of my closest friends in school, which he wasn't. So, out of curiosity, I asked him a question, "Hey Mike, I still don't understand how you have changed so much."

He smiled at me and responded, *"I used to think that everybody owes me something but now I don't think like that."* His brief answer didn't let me sleep at night. I kept on thinking about what he said. His answer made one thing clear; it's a person's way of thinking that makes him sociable. He changed his way of thinking, which made him a friendly person.

Since this book is about achieving success in career and life, which can be achieved easily if you have a friendly attitude towards people, I have done some research and collected some valuable information on how you can do that.

People who are friendly in nature think a certain way, which makes them a popular choice in every social situation. Here is how friendly people think. If you want to be sociable, you need to adopt these guidelines.

1: No Expectations from Others

The first thing you should do to develop sociability is to start having no expectations from others. Expectations are the only reason you hold grudges with other people. Also, having expectations make you feel hurt at some point, which reflects in your attitude towards others (the Zen Buddhists say that expectations bring suffering – when they are not met). Here is how you can train yourself to have no expectations from others.

- Think that nobody owes you anything. If a person doesn't respond to you the way you expected them to, then it's ok. He/she is not your slave and you are not his/hers. Just find someone else whom you really connect to.

- If you have done anyone a favor, then don't expect a return from him/her. The reason you gave him/her the favor is your reason not his/hers.

- Don't think that people will treat you nicely just because you are funny. Everybody has his/her own sense of humor. Accept that fact and move on.

2: Respect Other's Opinions

Everybody has its own opinion regarding something. If you disagree with someone's opinion, respect it and don't try to make fun of it to gain attention. It will not make you look friendly; rather, you will sound judgmental and nobody likes to share their stuff with people who are judgmental.

3: Be Natural

The most important factor of every friendly person you encounter is their commitment to themselves. They don't try acting differently in every social circle just to fit in; rather, they generally act natural. It's the best way you can come up friendly to others. However, if your natural self is to be judgmental all the time, you need to work on it because nobody likes the company of a judgmental person.

If you implement the above guidelines, you will undoubtedly notice an improvement in your life as far as your interaction with others is concerned. All this will help you to build good social and professional networks, which you can use to your advantage when necessary.

Conclusion

We have come to the end of the book. Thank you for reading and congratulations for reading until the end.

I truly hope you found the book helpful. As you implement what you have learned, keep in mind that you should combine all the above behaviors with discipline. Work on building discipline in your sleeping habits, taking care of your body (mental and physical health – including fitness), work life balance etc. And in so doing, you shouldn't have a hard time standing out in whatever you do.

I hope this book proves helpful in training yourself in achieving your career and life goals.

Good luck!

www.ingramcontent.com/pod-product-compliance
Lightning Source LLC
Chambersburg PA
CBHW031546210526
45464CB00003B/1178